A SPIRIT DAUGHTER WORKBOOK

WRITTEN BY
JILL WINTERSTEEN

FOR SCORPIO SEASON
OCTOBER 23RD - NOVEMBER 22ND

THE NEW MOON
MONDAY, NOVEMBER 13TH
1:27AM PT

PGS. 2-13: SCORPIO SEASON
PGS. 14-25: SCORPIO NEW MOON
PGS. 26-27: SCORPIO SIGN INFO
PGS. 28-29: ASTROLOGY FORECAST

SCORPIO SEASON

Scorpio Season is a magical time that brings us the opportunity to face our deepest shadows, accept them, and grow with them instead of away from them. This season teaches us how to become our own shamans, alchemists, and psychologists as we travel to the deepest layers of our beings. As the Sun sits in the energy of Scorpio, it brings us the courage to face our whole selves and a willingness to be honest about every aspect of our energy. This season feels very intense at times as we ride the waves of Scorpio, but the turmoil is worth it, as we discover forgotten pieces of our souls and heal the foundation of our hearts. As we begin this new season, take the calmness and balance you found in Libra and hold on to it. It is from this place of inner harmony that you can truly begin to do the work Scorpio Season offers. Return to your breath and your body when you need to, and always remember that you have the power to return to peace.

Ruled by Pluto and Mars, Scorpio brings us face to face with the raw truth of life. It brings up the more challenging topics of existence that we often choose to ignore simply because it's more comfortable. Avoidance, though, is not an option during Scorpio Season. Everything comes up to the surface, and we have the choice to either work with what is normally hidden or run from it. Unfortunately, running is an option for only so long. Eventually, our shadows catch up to us and we have to confront them one way or another. Scorpio Season is an opportunity to do deep shadow work before these energies meddle in our lives and block our highest intentions. It's a time to see what lies behind the curtain of our conscious minds and controls us from behind the scenes. Scorpio reminds us that whether we face them or not, hidden energies exist, bringing in self-doubt or sabotaging our efforts to manifest our lives. The only way to deal with these energies is to face them. Through this awareness we can accept them and transmute them. Only after we reveal our shadows are we are free to build our intentions on a sturdy foundation. This is the season for those revelations.

Shadow work is some of the deepest work we can do on ourselves. It is an integral part of any healing practice and a necessary complement to our spiritual endeavors. If we choose to leave out shadow work and focus on other modalities, we will end up in an infinite loop of repeating patterns. Only through going deep within and facing our darkest shadows can we break conditioned patterns or self-sabotaging cycles that block our highest potential. While shadow work needs to be done alongside other practices, it is essential for energetic transformation and evolution.

SCORPIO SEASON

Our shadow is where we place anything and everything that was too overwhelming, frightening, or intense when we originally experienced it. Most of our shadows were formed in childhood, but they can also be formed in adulthood. If, for instance, a child experiences an emotion they do not understand and they do not get guidance from a caregiver on how to process it—or worse, are punished for displaying that emotion—the child dissociates from that emotion. It then becomes part of the child's shadow. Our shadows also hold parts of ourselves we are ashamed of and cannot bear to face. We do not want to identify with these aspects of ourselves, so we separate from them by acting like they don't exist. When we look at our shadows from a compassionate viewpoint, we see that they are all the energies that we didn't have the ability to confront—the things that were too much for us to experience in the moment because we didn't have the tools to work with them. So we packed them away and placed them as far from our conscious identities as possible. The trick of the shadow, though, is that, as long as an energy remains there, it always has the ability to control us. It is attached to us and affects us until we unpack it and accept that it is part of us.

The first part of understanding your shadow is knowing that it remains with you at all times yet is just out of your conscious view. It works through your subconscious mind. Your shadow is responsible when you have an intense reaction to something and don't know why. It causes you to have subtle and subconscious facial expressions that reveal subconscious judgments. And it even causes you to become attracted to certain types of people who cause you to relive trauma. Your shadow wants to be seen, and Scorpio Season is the time see it. Working with your shadow, though, requires courage, support, and compassion. Before beginning shadow work, make sure you feel centered in your body. Use the tools you gained in Libra Season to bring yourself into balance. Also make a list of the people who support you. Try to have weekly talks with them about the work you are doing. Enlisting the support of a trusted therapist can also be beneficial when you are working with shadows, especially if they become overwhelming or take over the majority of your thoughts. Remember to have compassion for yourself during this work. Accepting your shadow without judgment is the key to transmuting it.

As you work with your shadows throughout Scorpio Season, be honest with yourself. Scorpio asks for the raw truth. Be willing to see and accept aspects of yourself that you'd rather hide. Explore your emotions with intense curiosity and without judgment. Acknowledge your pain, your shame, and your regrets. Notice and confront your triggers. If someone or something causes a reaction within you, ask yourself why and get ready for an honest answer. See every reaction as an opportunity to learn something about yourself and to form a new pattern. Also, when you experience one emotion, go deeper and find the emotion behind the feeling. Often when we experience an emotion, it is a reaction to a trigger. When we explore that emotion more, we find another emotion—the one we've been avoiding. This feeling is actually the primary or foundational emotion, which is the shadow. Notice if you have shame around experiencing the shadow emotion and hold space for yourself to explore it. As you get to the bottom of your emotions, you acquire the ability to transmute the energy into something else. This is where the alchemy of Scorpio shines. When you feel the thing you avoided feeling, you actually shift it into something else. You free the energy and allow it to become another version of itself. Scorpio is not about letting go, and neither is shadow work. It's about looking at what really is and shifting it into something that helps you become who you're meant to be.

TIPS FOR SCORPIO SEASON

TIPS FOR WORKING WITH YOUR SHADOWS

LOOK AT YOUR TRIGGERS

Your triggers are the largest keys to finding your shadows. When you experience an emotion or physical sensation that seems too large or out of place for the current situation, you may be peering into your shadow. A trigger can be anxiety or anger. It can also be a feeling of pressure or being overwhelmed. The key is that it doesn't belong to the present situation. The present is simply triggering your shadow to react and be seen. A trigger can also be external, like a person or event. It can even be a time of day or specific location. For instance, if you meet someone who looks like someone from the past and you immediately become angry with them, that may be your shadow showing up. Perhaps you dissociated from your initial anger, or the anger is the surface emotion. When you dig deeper, you may find sadness or even grief as the primary shadow emotion. It all starts by looking at what or who triggers reactions within you.

LOOK AT YOUR JUDGMENTS

The people we judge the most can often teach us about our shadows. What we despise or reject in another person is simply a mirror for what we despise and reject in ourselves. This pathway to our shadows can be a tough one because it can be very challenging to admit we share common energies with the people who trigger us the most. Often, though, those are the people who reflect our deepest shadows. The next time you are trigged by someone, try to have an imaginary conversation with them. You don't need to have a real conversation with them because that can become unproductive for shadow work. Instead, ask them questions in your head and await the answers. Find out what this person could teach or show you. You can even ask them why they trigger you so much. Ask them as many questions as you need to find out what they are reflecting back to you. What pieces of yourself are buried in this person and how can you accept them as part of yourself?

LOOK AT YOUR DREAMS

Sleep can provide a window into the subconscious, and often our shadows show up in our dreams or nightmares. Throughout Scorpio Season, create a dream journal. Write in it every morning upon waking. Even if you don't think you remember your dreams, still take out your journal and give yourself the space to remember. Amethyst is a wonderful stone to help you recall dreams. Sleep with one by your bedside or even under your pillow to facilitate dream recall. As you write about what you dreamed, notice any repeating patterns. Is the same monster always chasing you? Or do you always find yourself unable to scream? Perhaps your dreams reveal something positive about yourself that you have forgotten. Do you exude confidence in a new way through your dreams, or do you dream of people you want to be but who, in reality, you already are? You can also try having a conversation with people or monsters in your dreams. Just like in the previous tip, ask them what they are trying to show or teach you. You can also ask them what aspect of yourself they are trying to reveal or mirror.

ALLOW YOURSELF TO FEEL

Shadow work requires the ability to feel your emotions. Often, though, we do not allow ourselves to feel. We feel shame about our emotions or they feel too intense. When we do not allow ourselves to feel, we send those feelings right into our shadow, fueling it instead of unpacking it. When doing shadow work, tell yourself it's ok to feel anything. Be open to any emotion that comes up for you. If emotions become too intense, take a break. Rely on your support system or practices that bring you balance. Try, though, to sit with the emotion and learn from it instead of banishing it to the shadow. There is no shame in any emotion. You are human and have a wide variety of feelings. They do not make you unlovable, unworthy, or imperfect. Have compassion for any emotion that

TIPS FOR SCORPIO SEASON

TIPS FOR WORKING WITH YOUR SHADOWS

arises. It's ok to feel anything. It's what you do with that feeling that matters. Feelings need nurturing and acknowledgment to shift into something productive instead of destructive. Give feelings space to been seen this season. Accept them and know you can transform them.

LOOK FOR THE EMOTION BEHIND THE EMOTION
When you are experiencing emotions, sit with them and have a conversation with them just as you do with your other triggers. You may find the primary or foundational shadow emotion through this process. Often, what we initially feel in a circumstance is not the real emotion. It is the strategy we developed to deal with and avoid a shadow. Some of our emotions were simply survival mechanisms—and clever ones—but they are not the real emotion we detached from in the first place. For instance, if you were made to feel guilty for feeling sad as a child because it made one of your parents upset, you may have packed sadness away in your shadow. You dissociated from it and even removed your ability to feel sad. So, when a situation develops later in life that would elicit sadness, you feel anger instead. You get angry at the situation and may even project your anger onto other people. Or you become triggered when someone displays sadness. You may even get angry at them for feeling that way. If you sit down and talk with your anger and ask what it is teaching or showing you, you may find the sadness you packed away so long ago. Instead of feeling inappropriate anger, you may finally be able to feel sadness and accept that emotion as part of you. This process can work with a variety of emotions, but it starts with understanding that some emotions are simply strategies for avoiding other ones.

LOOK FOR THE LIGHTER SHADOWS
Shadows are not all dark. We also pack away some positive energies because they do not fit our ideas of ourselves. For instance, if you were taught that you would be cut off from your family if you demonstrated too much success or confidence, then your self-confidence or intellect may be in your shadow. You may then end up triggered by highly successful people, which shows you a shadow. Often we form identities of who we are that are based on who our families think we should be. We want to fit in with family lineage, and it can take years to realize our potential. Part of this process is shadow work. Know that some of the qualities you are trying to cultivate in yourself may already be part of you. You just cut yourself off from them. Recognize which higher energies you may have stored in your shadow and integrate them into who you are today.

OWN YOUR SHADOWS
In order to fully unpack our shadows and take away their ability to subconsciously control us, we must own them. We must accept them as part of ourselves and love them just as we love the rest of us. Our shadows represent our wounds, and they simply want to be acknowledged and loved. They may be the pieces of your psyche that feel out of place or unhinged, but what they really want is acceptance. Owning your shadows is the only way to ensure they don't sabotage your dreams, ruin your relationships, or take your energetic resources. When you accept and integrate your shadows, you free your energy to create your highest intentions. You can manifest your dreams without internal obstacles popping up to block you. You also know when your shadows are appearing, and you can handle them with care instead of projecting them onto people or situations. You live from your authentic truth and accept yourself. A bonus is that other people feel at ease around you because you've accepted the shadows of yourself and no longer judge others.

* Learn more about working with your shadows in the Scorpio Lunar Cycle Shadow Work Course.

HOROSCOPES

ARIES RISING: This season and New Moon affect your 8th house of personal growth. Expect this season to be full of transformational experiences, some of them unexpected. Enjoy making yourself, and your evolution, a priority. Say no to anything that doesn't fully resonate with you, always remembering that if it doesn't give you energy, it is taking it away. Gift yourself more time than usual each day in meditation and on the New Moon. Explore the inner workings of your mind and energy on a deeper level through journalling, diving into workshops, and simply giving yourself space to be.

TAURUS RISING: This season and New Moon affect your 7th house of partnerships. You may experience some shifts in your relationships. Be open to changes in this department, including saying goodbye to some partners. Remember that not everyone is meant to be in your life forever, some are, but some are here just until the karma is worked out. Recognize can relationships that need transformation, even if that just means having some honest, possibly uncomfortable conversations. Lean on your spiritual practices even more, to help steady you as you make shifts in your world.

GEMINI RISING: This season and New Moon affect your 6th house of service. Recognize how you need to change how you work with your talents. We all have a purpose this lifetime, but the mission or execution of that purpose changes over time. You may be due for a change in your work life or how you align with your soul's purpose. Become aware of any talents you may be hiding or not utilizing and give them attention. Bring your hidden gifts to the forefront of your consciousness and energy where everyone can see them.

CANCER RISING: This season and New Moon affect your 5th house of creativity. It's a time to go within and ask yourself what you are ready to create in your life. Spend time alone this season and give yourself space to experiment with new modalities that help bring your inner world to the exterior. Also, become aware of any vulnerability that surfaces when you think about sharing your creativity with the world. Acknowledge that energy and transform it. Use it to fuel your creativity and add more heart into it. Resist the urge to hold back this season and step forward into your life without hesitation.

LEO RISING: This season and New Moon affect your 4th house of the home. This is a quieter time than usual for you. Let yourself be a homebody and say no without guilt to any requests that don't fully resonate with your heart. Dive deep into the mysteries of your mind and energy. Be curious about yourself and your motives. Learn about yourself on a new level using methods of self-inquiry like journaling, workshops, and meditation. Experiment with new modalities of spiritual practices as you spend time in the foundation of yourself.

VIRGO RISING: This season and New Moon affect your 3rd house of communication. Become aware this season of the subtle ways you communicate with others. It's not always words that exchange energy with others. Notice how you use your posture, eyes, and even mouth movements to subtly convey information. Then become aware of how much of this subtle communication is unconscious and ask yourself how you can make it conscious. You may not always communicate what you want, or it may not be landing as you intend.

HOROSCOPES

LIBRA RISING: This season and New Moon affect your 2nd house of resources. It's time to shift your mindset around abundance and finances. Align with Scorpio to dig deep into any shadows you have in this area. Notice your triggers around things like debt, other people's finances, and your ability to create abundance. Transform how you think about your resources and acknowledge the energetic ones at your disposal. You have the power to create any form of abundance you desire. This season is a time to overcome any blocks in this area and free yourself to step into your most abundant self.

SCORPIO RISING: This season and New Moon affect your 1st house of identity. Over this season, notice what you are projecting into the world with your energy. Ask yourself if this is how you want people to see you and if this energy represents the real you. Align with Scorpio to understand your unconscious ego attachments. Then dissolve these attachments by understanding that you do not need to be anything to be everything. You are one with the Universe and do not need to fit into any one box. Re-invent yourself this season if needed, and know that no one determines who you are except you.

SAGITTARIUS RISING: This season and New Moon affect your 12th house of spirituality. Let yourself wander into the mysteries of your mind and energy this season. Read books that inspire you and teach you about yourself. Learn new spiritual practices like different forms of meditation, energetic bodywork, and yoga. Be open to serendipity and signs from the Universe pointing you to new spiritual paths. Let yourself transform again and again this season until you feel your energy's infinite and limitless potential.

CAPRICORN RISING: This season and New Moon affect your 11th house of community. You may find yourself gathering with others more frequently than usual this season. These acquaintances, some of them new, will help you open new doors to understanding your unconscious layers. Let others act as a mirror for you, and you learn something new about yourself this season. Honor the interconnectedness of all beings and see yourself in everyone you meet. Be the teacher and student of life this season as you let others help you transform into the next version of yourself.

AQUARIUS RISING: This season and New Moon affect your 10th house of career. You may find yourself going through shifts in your work life this season. Know that it's all for the best, and any detours are an upgrade, even if they don't seem that way at first. This is a season of growth. Some of that growth may evolve you into a new career path. Be cautious not to hold onto something that has lived past its prime. If you don't graciously release it when needed, it will be forced out of your hands. Recognize what needs to change in your work life and make steps to shift it this season.

PISCES RISING: This season and New Moon will affect your 9th house of knowledge. You may take a trip or at least plan one this season. You may also find yourself exploring new realms of knowledge, mysticism, and magic. This is a time of profound exploration for you, both of yourself and the world around you. Plunge into the deep end of your emotions, energy, and love for all things mysterious. Experiment with new spiritual practices, read books on energetics and learn even more about astrology. Let your attention wander and follow it. Also, look for direction from the Universe. If a path is glowing, follow it.

CRYSTALS FOR SCORPIO

SNOWFLAKE OBSIDIAN is known as a stone of purity. It cleanses the mind, body, and energy of any negativity and brings balance to the wearer. It is an excellent grounding stone, connecting to the energy of the root chakra. Hold a piece when you are feeling insecure or unstable. Snowflake obsidian also holds the vibration of reflection. It will reflect the energetic frequency you are holding. Through this mirroring, it helps you shift your energy and transform it into something else.

Snowflake Obsidian vibrates to the mantra: I am grounded.

RAINBOW HEMATITE is a stone of balance. Its magnetic properties help balance the energetic systems of the body and bring grounding to the spirit. Through this balance, hematite helps filter the mind's thoughts, sorting out what information is important and what is coming from a place of fear or anxiety. Hold a piece when you need to feel grounded and focused. It will also bring about a sense of calmness. Rainbow Hematite is metallic in color.

Rainbow Hematite vibrates to the mantra: I am calm, cool, and collected.

ONYX is a stone of magic. It has been used for centuries in rituals, healing practices, and ceremonies. It encourages alignment with your highest powers and gives you clearer access to your visions. Onyx also helps you recognize your power while grounding your energy so you may use it. It is a powerful stone and a beautiful addition to any circle or altar space. Have some near when you are practicing rituals or want to access your powers of transformation.

Onyx vibrates to the mantra: I am powerful.

RUBY FUCHSITE helps you open your heart and dive deeper into your truth, including your truth about yourself. It also helps remove barriers around the heart space, facilitating the transmission of unconditional love both to yourself and others. Hold some in your hand to give yourself support when doing shadow work. Feel into your love for yourself no matter what Scorpio Season reveals, and know that by maintaining an open heart, you keep the connection to your intuition open.

Ruby Fuchsite vibrates to the mantra: I am loved.

SCOCELITE facilitates deep spiritual transformation. It brings about peace and inner calm during times of change and can even help with sleep when the mind is overactive. Place some under your pillow if cascading thoughts wake you in the night. It is also great to have near while journaling or meditating as you navigate unknown territory.

Scocelite vibrates to the mantra: I am at peace with change.

SCORPIO MEDITATION

KAPALABHATI PRANAYAMA

Focusing and altering our breath is one of the tools of alchemy we possess. Breathwork is relatively easy, and you can do it anywhere. Kapalabhati, or breath of fire, is an ancient yogic breathwork that helps purify your energetic body. It also brings in new, fresh energy you can work with and circulate throughout your body. Practice this every day throughout Scorpio Season to help process and digest all the information being brought to you. This breathwork will also transmute feelings of heaviness into lightness, giving you the perfect tool when your breath becomes stagnant or the energy around you feels too intense.

Sit in a comfortable position with your spine straight. You can sit on a cushion or pillow to elevate your hips higher than your knees. Relax your shoulders but feel your core supporting your spine. Close your eyes and take a deep inhale, then exhale. On your next inhale, fill up only two-thirds of the way with air. On exhale, take short, sharp exhales out through your nose while pumping your belly. It will feel like you are attempting to blow out a candle with your exhale. Focus solely on your exhales, allowing the inhales to come naturally. Continue this for 50 rounds of exhales. Afterward, take a deep inhale and hold your breath for a count of 10, then exhale slowly. Repeat the entire sequence for a second time. Once you finish both sets, allow your breath to become natural. Feel into the expansion you've created and observe the feeling of new energy circulating throughout your system.

MICROCOSMIC ORBIT MEDITATION
(Please also listen to the audio version of this meditation)

This meditation is an ancient Qigong technique. It helps circulate your energy and free up any blockages causing stagnation. When you move your energy, you provide space for it to transmute. Practice this meditation every day during Scorpio Season to unblock your energy, allowing it to shift and change.

For the first round, you will spend two breaths in each area. After the first round, the pace will quicken. Envision a golden light, like the Sun, above your head. Imagine a pearl of sunshine from this light dropping down to your third eye. Feel it warm this area and soften it. Now send the pearl of light to the tip of your tongue. As it moves, feel its warmth and light opening up each area it touches. Send the pearl down your throat, opening and harmonizing it. Continue the pearl down the front of your body to your heart center. Feel the pearl sending light to your heart, opening and healing it. Now send the pearl to your navel, relaxing your abdomen. Send the pearl down to the base of your pelvis. Have the pearl make a loop around your torso, moving up the back of your body. Move it first to the sacrum (the triangular bone at the base of your spine). Move the pearl up to your kidneys, replenishing them. Continue the pearl up your spine to the back of your heart as you feel your entire body soften. Next, bring it to the base of your skull. Move the pearl up the back of your skull, awakening your ability to see in every direction. Finally, bring it through the top of your head, pausing at the crown and inviting in information.

Return the pearl to the third eye, where you began. This is one round. The subsequent rounds will move with your breath. On inhale, pass the pearl down the front of your body, through each point, to the base of your pelvis. On exhale, pump the pearl up the back of your body to the crown of your head. Continue this circuit for 5 minutes. Watch the pearl go round and round, lighting up the areas it touches and bringing movement to your energy. When you are finished, slowly open your eyes and feel into the rest of your body. Move your hands and feet, giving them attention and energy. Sense your entire being awakened and energized.

SCORPIO LUNAR FLOW

Scorpio rules the hips and pelvis, which is the seat of creativity. Her energy is fluid, as she is water, and reminds us to move our bodies with ease and grace. By softly opening our bodies, we can move stagnant energy and release blocks against our own evolution. This sequence is designed to put you in touch with the natural rhythm of your energy and encourage it to flow evenly through your whole being. Practice it throughout Scorpio Season and on her New Moon.

THREAD-THE-NEEDLE POSE

Begin with your back on your mat. Bend both knees and cross your left ankle over your right knee, making a four with your legs. Thread your left arm through the hole of the four and grasp your right hand around your right shin, picking up that leg. Make sure your neck is relaxed; use a pillow under your head if needed. Breathe here for 5 deep breaths, sending each inhale down into your hips and releasing the tension on the exhale. Then switch sides.

SEATED SEQUENCE

Come up to a cross-legged position. With your spine upright, make circles in your hips, rolling your torso around. Continue this for about 30 seconds, then switch directions. Feel the fluid movement of your body.

Come back to center and interlace your hands behind your head. On inhale, twist to the right. Exhale, twist to the left. Do this for 1 minute, then release.

Still seated, place your hands on your knees, then arch and round your back. Feel the full undulation of your spine as it waves back and forth. Even feel your neck and throat open as you arch your spine. Continue for 1 minute, then return to stillness.

CAT/COW TO DOWNWARD-FACING DOG

Come onto your hands and knees. Arch your back on inhale, then round it on exhale. Again, feel the wave of your spine and the fluidity of your movement. Continue for 1 minute. Come back to center and roll through your rib cage, making large circles with your torso. Continue for 30 seconds before switching sides. There is no right or wrong way to do these; just move organically and in tune with your body. Come back to center and exhale into Downward Dog.

* Visit spiritdaughter.com/collections/zodiac-yoga to flow with our Scorpio Zodiac Yoga video.

SCORPIO LUNAR FLOW

SUN SALUTATION A - 5 ROUNDS

Stand at the top of your mat. Inhale, stretch your arms overhead > Exhale, fold forward > Inhale, lengthen out your back > Exhale, step back to Plank Pose and lower > Inhale, reach your chest up for Cobra Pose, legs on the ground > Exhale, Downward Dog. Stay here for 5 breaths and feel your entire body expand. On Exhale, step to the top of your mat > Inhale, lengthen through your spine > Exhale, fold forward > Inhale, come up to standing, reaching arms overhead > Exhale, hands to your heart. Pause for a moment and feel yourself centered throughout your body.

On your fifth round, remain in Downward Dog and breathe for 5 breaths.

LUNGE > WARRIOR 2 > GODDESS POSE

From Downward Dog, step your left foot forward into a Lunge Pose. Your back heel will lift from the ground and your leg will stay straight. Bend deeply into your front knee as you tilt your tailbone toward the ground. Reach your arms to the sky and send your breath into your hips. After 5 breaths, open up into Warrior 2. Spin your back foot flat inward on the ground at a 45-degree angle and rotate your torso to the right side of your mat, reaching your arms to either side. Bend in your front knee, pressing it out to the left. Take 5 breaths here, opening up your pelvis and grounding down through your legs. Inhale, straighten your leg, and bring your feet to parallel in a wide-legged stance. Turn your toes out to a 45-degree angle and bend in your knees for Goddess Pose. Bend your arms by your sides with your palms facing the sky. Breathe here for 5 breaths as you feel your feet root into the ground. Once complete, straighten your legs and rotate your right foot out, repeating Warrior 2 and Lunge on this side. From Warrior 2, release your hands to the ground and step back through a Vinyasa or straight to Downward Dog.

MALASANA (SQUAT POSE)

Hop your feet forward to the outside of your hands with your feet hips width or wider and your toes slightly turned out. Drop your hips down for a Squat Pose. Press firmly through the outer edges of your feet and feel your heels energetically draw together. If your heels lift from the ground, place a blanket beneath them or sit on a block until your hips release and open. Take 5 deep breaths here, allowing your hips to open as your feet root into the Earth. Release into a forward bend, hanging over your legs as your spine releases.

PIGEON POSE

Return to Downward Dog through a Vinyasa or by stepping back and taking your left knee to your left wrist for Pigeon Pose. Go easy on your knee. If you feel any pain, return to Thread the Needle. Carefully lay down your left leg and stretch your right leg back. Before folding, press up through your hands and arch your back a bit, stretching through the front of your body. On exhale, fold forward over your leg and remain here for 10 breaths. On each inhale, send your breath into your hips, encouraging them to open. On exhale, release a bit more. After 10 breaths, slowly switch sides.

SAVASANA

Release to the floor, lying with your palms up and your eyes closed. Feel your body alive with fresh energy circulating throughout your system. Feel the ground beneath you supporting you. Know this support is always available to you from Mother Earth. Rest here fully for 5 minutes.

THE NEW MOON

NOVEMBER 13TH

The New Moon is a time of new beginnings. On this day, the Sun and Moon meet in the sky in the same zodiac sign. They rise and set at the same time, syncing their energy and their vibration. The Sun and Moon's conjunction, and lack of sunlight on the Moon, makes the Moon appear invisible to us. Even if we could see her, it would only be during daytime hours as she travels the sky with the Sun. On the night of the New Moon, only stars light the sky and we are left with the darkest time of the lunar cycle.

Darkness is often thought of as a negative period, but it is neither positive nor negative. Darkness represents the void from which all life and energy spring, as it is the seat of creativity. When we close our eyes or enter a dark space, the imagination flourishes and we gain access to our inner worlds. Darkness is also calming to our energy and nervous system. It helps the mind quiet, and in that space, intuition becomes louder. We can hear our inner guidance and receive answers instead of searching for them. We can peer into the subconscious at a deeper level. When we meditate, for instance, we travel into darkness as we close our eyes and reduce sensory input from the external world. In this place, we can broaden our internal senses to feel patterns of behavior and conditioning buried deep below the conscious mind. We can see our blocks and shadows, but we can also see our dreams and true desires. Darkness gives us a greater view of who we are and what we want in this world.

Each New Moon becomes a time to align with the darkness of the night and travel to the center of yourself. This is where you can discover your hopes, dreams, fears, and underlying patterns. Each month, with the help of the New Moon, you have an opportunity to learn about yourself on a deeper level. You can more easily hear your intuition and its guidance on where to set intentions, redefine yourself, and shift patterns. It is also a gentle reminder to check in with yourself to see how you are progressing with your visions and to fine-tune the energy you need to manifest your intentions with greater success.

The New Moon provides further guidance based on the zodiac sign she and the Sun are traveling through, or transiting. Each month, the New Moon is themed by this astrological energy. This zodiac vibration is what creates subtle, but noticeable, differences in each New Moon. This transit also provides a blueprint on what to work on in our energy and what to write intentions around. This month, the Moon and Sun meet in the stars of Scorpio, giving us the theme of transformation. The intuitive guidance we receive and the supporting energy of this Moon lead the way to transmuting our shadows into our strengths.

The astrological theme of the New Moon is the same for all of us, no matter where you live in the world or what your Sun sign is. It is universal and unifying. We all feel the effects of Scorpio's energy this New Moon, and we all can work with this energy in our personal lives. Where you'll feel Scorpio and the New Moon's energy the greatest depends on the house in which the New Moon is transiting for you. You can find which of your houses is most affected by this New Moon by pulling your natal chart at astro-charts.com. Locate the house, or houses, ruled by Scorpio. Here you will find the area of your life most affected by the New Moon and the area where your intentions can manifest to the greatest degree. For instance, if Scorpio rules your Third House of Communication, this New Moon is an excellent time for you to look at your exchanges of energy. Focus on this area to find patterns that can be shifted into strengths instead of blocks. On the opposite page is a list of what to focus on this New Moon according to which house is ruled by Scorpio in your natal chart.

THE NEW MOON

NOVEMBER 13TH

SCORPIO IN THE:	FOCUS ON:
1ST HOUSE	Focus on transforming the ways you present yourself to the world.
2ND HOUSE	Focus on transforming how you view possessions and your relationship with your worth.
3RD HOUSE	Focus on transforming how you communicate and exchange energy.
4TH HOUSE	Focus on transforming your deepest, most subjective emotions.
5TH HOUSE	Focus on transforming your relationship with your inner child.
6TH HOUSE	Focus on transforming how you view your talents and gifts.
7TH HOUSE	Focus on transforming how you show up in partnerships.
8TH HOUSE	Focus on your personal growth.
9TH HOUSE	Focus on transforming how you approach novel experiences.
10TH HOUSE	Focus on transforming your career.
11TH HOUSE	Focus on transforming your energetic participation in the collective.
12TH HOUSE	Focus on transforming through spiritual growth and meditation.

You may also feel the effects of this New Moon at areas of chart where you have planets around 20°. This New Moon occurs when the Sun and Moon meet at 20° Scorpio. There are 30 degrees in a sign, totaling 360°. If you happen to have any planets within 15° and 25° Scorpio, you will feel the energies of that planet intensify in your personality and energetic field on the Full Moon. If you have any planets between 15 and 25° Leo, Aquarius, or Taurus, you may feel a breakthrough with these energies. At first you may experience some tension in those aspects of your energy, but the New Moon will open a pathway forward to a new perspective. If you have any planets between 15° and 25° Cancer, Pisces, Virgo, or Capricorn, you will feel those energies enhanced in your field. They may start to make more sense, or they may even help you form intentions or work with shadows this New Moon. Understanding your natal chart is just one way to work more deeply with the energy of the cosmos. Look at these places in your chart this New Moon and expand your understanding of your own knowledge.

---

* You can learn more about your personal natal chart and houses in the 3-Part Natal Chart Series available on spiritdaughter.com.

SCORPIO X THE NEW MOON

NOVEMBER 13TH

The Scorpio New Moon is a time of profound emotional transformation. Scorpio helps us understand our hidden truths, including our unconscious patterns and desires. The New Moon helps us plant seeds of intention for new beginnings. In Scorpio, the New Moon helps us define the truth we want to live. It's a time to express what we need, desire, and are ready for in our lives. It's also a time to listen to the truth of our intuition. Scorpio heightens both our emotions and intuitive knowing this New Moon, giving us the keys to crafting a new vision for the future.

As you work with the energy of this New Moon, know that it may sometimes feel intense. This New Moon brings up many feelings, some of which may surprise you. If you suddenly cry, scream, or even emotionally withdraw, give yourself space to process your feelings. You may not understand them at first, but with time and attention, they will make sense. This New Moon may also bring up underlying emotions usually buried in your shadows or unconscious mind. Scorpio makes the unconscious conscious. Let this Moon reveal buried truths. Often what you feel is just the surface. Dig deep this Moon to find what lies beneath the surface. If you are feeling something, ask if there is something underneath that feeling or if it is masking another emotion.

Let this New Moon help you understand a deeper layer of yourself. Notice if you have any fear around diving into the deep end of your soul. Does this emotional work make you feel vulnerable? Or perhaps ungrounded? Steady yourself by connecting with your body through movement and breath. Feel layers release and transform as you remain curious about all of them. As you plunge into your psyche, resist the urge to hold back because of fear. Feel your strength and your power to transform any emotion into something else. The Scorpio New Moon is an opportunity to be your own alchemist. If you feel an intense emotion, think of it as energy. Then feel into the emotion and decide what else you can do with that energy. What can you transform it into to help your journey instead of hinder it?

As you peel back the layers of emotion this New Moon, you unlock hidden doorways to your intuition. You always know exactly what to do when you need to do it. You just need to learn to listen to yourself. Unprocessed or suppressed emotions, though, can block your inner knowing. As you write intentions for this New Moon, follow your intuition. Let your inner truth guide you. Do not question it, do not ask for logical steps or proof, and do not ignore it. Listen to your intuition and let it help you define and new reality, one that is based in your present energy, not your past definitions.

SCORPIO X THE NEW MOON

NOVEMBER 13TH

ASPECTS

There are a few aspects this New Moon adding to the energy of the day. The Sun and Moon are conjunct, or next to, Mars in Scorpio. Mars is the traditional planetary ruler of Scorpio and one of the rulers, along with Pluto, of this New Moon. Mars adds fire and even more intensity to this New Moon. You may feel anger, frustration, or restlessness arise. These emotions may illuminate places where your boundaries have been infringed upon.

Boundaries and anger are energetically tied together. When someone crosses our boundaries, or we have trouble setting them in the first place, we feel anger. Anger itself is often the first sign that your boundaries need some attention. Setting boundaries, though, is often challenging. We may even have shadows or unconscious patterns that cause us not to set them. When we don't set boundaries, we don't honor who we are and our inherent truth. Defining boundaries and sticking to them helps us protect ourselves and also protects the life we are creating. Over this New Moon, acknowledge where you need boundaries to honor your energy and growth. Also, notice if you have anger or frustration and then ask how they can inform you need boundaries.

The Moon, Sun, and Mars all oppose Uranus Retrograde in Taurus as well this New Moon. Uranus is the planet of change and helps us break up old patterns in our energy and behavior. Like all breakthroughs, though, there is often a preceding breakdown that occurs. If you experience strong emotions that feel like they are melting your soul, be aware of what is breaking through. Acknowledge old patterns that don't honor your feelings or push them aside. Instead, challenge yourself to sit with the intensity of your feelings and let them teach you. When an intense emotion arises, ask yourself what the emotion is helping you break through and what is helping you understand about yourself.

Uranus also helps us form new visions of the future. This is a very creative planet and brings out our visionary senses. After we muddle through the emotions and breakthroughs this New Moon brings us, we can feel our creativity and visionary intuition. Scorpio reminds us that we are the creators of our reality. We can create any dream through energetic intention and focus. For true creativity to flourish, though, we need to dissolve old patterns that hold us back.

Creativity of any kind feels like a risk. When we create something new, whether a piece of art or a new life, we venture into the unknown. We leave what feels familiar, and we journey into new territory. As you dissolve old patterns this New Moon, notice how it feels to be in the space of not knowing. When we exist in the in-between, it can feel scary. We may want to run back to what feels comfortable while simultaneously knowing our only choice is to move forward through the unknown. To create a new life, vision, or pattern, we have to leave the old behind and be ok with the uncomfortableness of the unknown.

Embrace this state of not knowing this New Moon, and remember that your intuition always knows the path forward. Be open to your visionary senses opening up to reveal the higher meaning of your life. Feel the expansiveness of your energy and its potential. Feel its reach and interconnectedness to so much more than just your life. Although the layers of this New Moon show you the full potential of your vibration this lifetime and from this vision, create intentions that call in the reality of your soul.

SETTING UP FOR MAGIC

Each zodiac sign carries inherent energy. With this energy comes colors, shapes, scents, and elements that match the sign's vibration. For every New Moon, we want to incorporate as many of these frequencies as possible. While none of them is required for aligning with the energy of the New Moon, they do help reflect the energy. Think of it as placing energetic mirrors around the room that help amplify and direct the energy. Use your intuition to guide the choice and placement of objects. Resist the urge to overthink where they belong. Let the crystals, in particular, choose their location. All you need to do is listen.

Pick a space, either inside or outside, that feels centered and stable. Imagine a white light creating the circle's boundary, then place candles, crystals, and other items within this boundary. Place a crystal, candle, or other piece of magic in the center to give structure to the circle. The center is also an excellent place to set up a crystal grid to direct the energy further. If you are creating an altar, you can place it in the easterly corner to help call in the energy of new beginnings. Know that your attention and awareness of the energy available is the most important thing for working with it. You can practice the exercises in this workbook in any way you choose; you can practice alone or in a group of people around a bonfire. Your willingness to open up, look within, and expand your consciousness is the most essential piece.

The other pieces for calling in and aligning with the energy of Scorpio are listed below. You can combine them in any way you like.

FOR YOUR ALTAR OR MOON CIRCLE

FLOWERS:
Hibiscus, Geranium, Musk, Saffron, Vanilla

COLORS:
Black, Dark Blues, Purples

TEXTURES/FABRIC:
Velour, Brushed Silk

SCENTS:
White Musk, Jasmine, Grapefruit

SHAPES:
Crescent

ELEMENTS:
Oracle/Tarot Cards,
Bowl of Water

Also incorporate the four elements in your circle. Use candles for Fire, a room diffuser or spray for Air, and the crystals and flowers for Earth. And have some water in a metal bowl. Once you set up your circle, cleanse the space with a dried herb bundle of your choice. Rosemary or cedar is wonderful for this New Moon. You can also use a space-clearing spray derived from essential oils. After the circle is cleansed, cleanse yourself and your friends before they enter the circle.

You can begin the circle by acknowledging everyone in the room. You can then continue to the yoga, if you are practicing, then the meditation. Once you feel the room is centered, talk about the astrology of the day and what it means for each of you. If it is a larger circle, you may want to designate a talking stick or crystal that each guest holds while they speak. After you've shared your understandings, continue with the questions in the workbook and the journaling portion. After

SETTING UP FOR MAGIC

everyone has finished, talk again about your experiences with the energy and the revelations that may have occurred. You can share as little or as much as you like with the group. Never feel obligated to speak; sometimes energies need time to develop before they are brought to light. At this point, you may also pull some cards to help tune further into your intuitive guidance. You can use tarot cards, goddess cards, animal medicine cards, or any other decks in your toolkit.

Once you've finished the circle, close it by having everyone close their eyes and meditate on what they are grateful for tonight and every night. You can even practice being grateful for things that haven't come your way yet. Gratitude will attract them to your energy and let the Universe know you are ready to receive them. Enjoy this time to be with yourself, your heart, and your soul. Get to know yourself on a deeper level and allow your life to unfold another layer each New Moon.

feel your power to shift from one vibration to another.

-spirit daughter

NEW MOON QUESTIONS

These questions are designed to help you become clear in your intentions. Take a few deep breaths to ground yourself before answering them. Sit with each question for a moment and allow the answer to naturally arise, being open to the person you are becoming. As you write, know you are opening the door to your intuition and giving permission to your highest visions to come out and be seen.

1. What helps you process emotions as they become intense?

2. What emotions are you ready to transform into something else? What are you transforming them into?

3. What would you do if fear didn't stop you?

4. What reality are you ready to create? What can help you believe in your power to create this reality?

INTENTION SETTING

Now is the time to plant your intentions for this lunar cycle. Some of these intentions will come to fruition by the next Full Moon in two weeks; others will come into your world over the next six months by the Full Moon in Scorpio in 2024. Your intentions help change your energetic vibration to tune into what you want. It's not about creating a wish list or a to-do list. Intentions help us hold the space for the vibrations we need to create our highest visions. They help us set the frequency, then we naturally attract that frequency into our lives. Intentions help us become our manifestations even before those manifestations appear in our lives.

Intentions also provide a guide for your attention if you feel lost during this lunar cycle. You can always come back to your intentions if you feel overwhelmed or drift away from them. Some intentions will usher in new behaviors, while others will serendipitously bring you new experiences and encounters that will propel you forward on your path.

It's most beneficial to create intentions around your personal growth and path of transformation on the Scorpio New Moon. These intentions can include seeing yourself respond or react in a different way. They may also include a vision of the life available to you past your shadows. It can be challenging to see your future self, but know that energy has no timeline. The future is already the present. When you write intentions, you are not seeing the future. You are seeing the present. As you write them, you are creating them. They exist the moment you visualize and write them down on paper. All you need to do is tune into their energy and become them.

Take a moment and create a scene in your mind. In this scene, all that you wish to call in is already yours. All you desire to change has already occurred. Do not worry about how you will get there or the list of to-dos needed to accomplish your goals. Just focus on the feeling of already living your dream. Know with every ounce of your being that it is already true; it already exists for you. Also, be open to the Universe giving detail to your visions. Allow flashes of intuition and brilliance to enter your space. Also, allow your shadows that block these intentions to show themselves. Hold space for them and accept them. Then envision who you are without them holding you back or keeping you small.

Write in as much detail as possible, and write without limits. Just let your mind explore. Align with the energy of Scorpio to clarify your dreams. What are you transforming with your words? What energy are you tuning into and calling in? What visions are creating in reality with your intentions? As you write, feel a sense of gratitude for what you are dreaming; thank the Universe for giving it to you, and thank yourself for creating it. Also hold space in your life for your dreams to evolve. Create openings for new experiences and realities. Let go of assumptions and expectations and instead allow the Universe to surprise you.

_____

_____

_____

_____

_____

_____

INTENTION SETTING

AFFIRMATIONS

The Scorpio New Moon is a powerful day to create new patterns of response in your life. First though, you must become aware of and call out the current patterns dictating your reactions and behavior. Most of us have old mantras we were taught at an early age that control our lives from behind the scenes. The key to transforming your energy is releasing these outdated mantras and replacing them with new ones that you can consciously control. When writing these new mantras, look to the house where this New Moon falls for you to find some guidance on where to focus your attention. For instance, if Scorpio contact your 10th house, look for programming around your life's work. What do you tell yourself about these things daily? Below write down your old programming. These can be things like "I am afraid" or "What if?" or "I'm not capable." or "I have to do…" Then rewrite your old mantras into new ones that oppose and challenge the old ones. Repeat your new affirmations daily until the next New Moon. Repetition is the key to new programming.

Affirmation Guidance:

+ Write them in "I am" statements.
+ Make them positive. Meaning, do not include no or not in them. The Universe doesn't hear the negative words, so keep them out of your affirmations.
+ Put them in the present tense. It can be tempting to put them in the future because that's when your conscious mind thinks they will happen. By making them in the present tense, you are letting your mind know they are already happening.
+ Make them specific. Write them in detail while also making them brief and powerful.
+ Include a feeling word. When you include a feeling word, it makes you feel. When you feel your affirmations, your energy starts to feel they are real and begins manifesting them.
+ Repeat them for thirty days. There is a special response in the brain that occurs when we do something for thirty days. The affirmation becomes real in our minds and energy.
+ For example: "I am celebrating the success of my new project with friend over dinner."

Scorpio

PERCEPTIVE. DETERMINED. INTUITIVE. FEARLESS.

PERSONAL SIGNS

SCORPIO SUN

People with Sun in Scorpio dive into the depths of life. They seek to understand everything at its most fundamental level. Whether this is themselves, the people in their lives, or an abstract subject, Scorpios want to get to the truth of the matter. They have the keen ability to focus on something for long periods and remember even the smallest details. Often called obsessive, Scorpios strive to know the ins and outs of whatever catches their current interest.

Ruled by Water, Scorpios are naturally emotional and intuitive. They hold a profound psychic ability that can take them a lifetime to understand and trust. Even as children, Scorpios have a deep knowing about themselves and are often described as "old souls." The challenge for Scorpios is to learn to trust their inner knowing. If they do not honor their intuition, they often feel betrayed and suffer greatly. Ignoring their intuitive knowledge leads to a life full of "what ifs" and anxiety as they seek to find answers outside themselves. All a Scorpio needs to do is tune into themself, and everything they seek will appear in their conscious mind.

Scorpios must learn to feel their way through life. They are on a quest to understand themselves on the deepest level. This understanding requires intense introspection and the courage to face parts of themselves that may not be so easy to digest. They have a deep need to know themselves, though. If they resist this desire, they can end up spinning their wheels, wandering from one direction to another, never knowing their purpose. One of Scorpio's resources is the ability to remain in the present moment long enough to understand it. Through watching themselves in the present, they can uncover mysteries about themselves. Once they distract themselves from the here and now, they lose the ability to dive deeper into their psyches. Scorpios are on a quest this lifetime to unravel their inner knowledge, understand their deepest layers, and feel their intuition at the bottom of it all, leading them out of the shadows and into the light.

SCORPIO MOON:

People with their Moon in Scorpio feel intensely. They invite emotion in so they can study it, understand it, and own it. They are on a journey to master their emotions while feeling them all. If they avoid or suppress their emotions, they end up feeling overwhelmed and unable to manage their many feelings.

Scorpio Moons need to set aside time to explore their many layers. This time and space is their form of self-care. They often need a special place at home where they can sit, meditate, and journal in peace, undisturbed by anyone else. Essentially they need a cave they can go into to wade through the many energies they experience daily.

When given the proper time and space to explore their emotions, they can become quite powerful. Scorpio Moons have a heightened intuition. When they can easily connect with it, they know exactly what to do and when to do it. Scorpio Moons are on a quest to understand everything about themselves. On this quest, they discover how to use their power. If they don't take this mission seriously and avoid their internal landscape, they can end up feeling moody, needy, and obsessive. If this low vibration occurs, it's best for Scorpio Moons to take time to meditate and listen to the wisdom they hold in each of their cells.

ASTROLOGY FORECAST

OCTOBER 28TH - NOVEMBER 20TH

OCTOBER 28TH: TAURUS LUNAR ECLIPSE
Please refer to the Taurus Lunar Eclipse Workbook

NOVEMBER 4TH: SATURN DIRECT IN PISCES
Saturn stations direct today, highlighting its energy. Saturn is the planet of responsibility and karma. Feel what and who you are responsible to today. In Pisces, Saturn reminds us to be accountable for our dreams. It also helps us weed out what is fantasy or illusion and what is a true vision. Be deliberate today in committing to visions that resonate with your soul. Be aware of any illusions that distract you from your truth. Instead, place boundaries around those distractions, not allowing them to steer you away from your soul's karmic path.

Also, notice what rules and restrictions are being placed or enforced within technology around today. Saturn in Pisces has been stirring up collective conversations around artificial intelligence, video streaming, virtual reality, and other technology that takes us into the future. Like many new systems, these systems have yet to be clearly defined. Saturn in Pisces is helping us create containers around them and understand their place in our society. This energy of Saturn will also be amplified today and the days leading to this direct station.

NOVEMBER 5TH: LAST QUARTER MOON IN LEO
Today we have the Last Quarter Moon, a time to fully release and create space before the Moon is new again. This Moon lands in the fierce, brave-hearted Leo, who always brings us to the heart of the matter. The pairing of the Moon and Leo and Sun and Scorpio gives us the courage to explore the deepest parts of ourselves and let go of what no longer serves our highest potential.

Today is a powerful time to shed layers we've lived with for years out of familiarity and fear of the unknown. Know that in letting go of thoughts, feelings, and situations, you are telling the Universe that you are ready to receive something different. Ask yourself tonight how you can face your deepest fears with love and compassion. How can you shift them into a higher vibration? Know that the Moon is helping you on the continuous journey of your soul's evolution.

NOVEMBER 8TH: VENUS ENTERS LIBRA
Venus returns to one of her homes today, Libra, until December 4th. Venus is the planet of love and beauty. It reminds us to work on our relationship with these things. This transit is a good time to ask yourself how you prioritize what you love in your life. It's also a good time to incorporate more beauty into your life. Shower yourself with things that make you feel good and remind you of the beauty of life. This may be fresh flowers on your altar each week, time spent in the beauty of nature, or new crystals to light up your meditation corner and inspire you. Focus on what opens your heart and pulls your attention to the radiance of life itself.

ASTROLOGY FORECAST

OCTOBER 28TH - NOVEMBER 20TH

NOVEMBER 9TH: MERCURY ENTERS SAGITTARIUS

Mercury joins the Sun in the expansive vibrations of Sagittarius today until December 1st. Mercury's time in Sagittarius expands us through communication. It's a time to exchange energies with others and learn from them. In Sagittarius, Mercury provides the opportunity to process ideas and concepts at a rapid rate. Be open to new information and energetic downloads, and listen to others when they tell their stories.

NOVEMBER 20TH: FIRST QUARTER MOON IN AQUARIUS

It's been one week since the New Moon. Now it's time to build our intentions and lay the foundation for them to manifest. Staying focused can be challenging, especially with so many distractions around. The First Quarter Moon asks us to stay committed to our paths and say no to anything that takes us away from them.

Coupled with Aquarius, the Moon today inspires us to connect with new ways of aligning with our visions. How can you re-envision obstacles or overcome blocks that may have popped up? Aquarius reminds us that there are many ways to solve a problem. It's all a matter of how we look at it.

Feel into your resounding yeses today and feel how you can send them energy. How can you carry the vibration of your visions and say no to anything that's not aligned with them? If you find yourself at a roadblock, harness the energy of Aquarius to create a unique solution to turn your block into a stepping stone.

UP NEXT
SAGITTARIUS SEASON

NOVEMBER 22ND

It's time to shake things up and take the road less traveled as we move into the adventurous energy of Sagittarius.

PURCHASE AT SPIRITDAUGHTER.COM

HAPPY NEW MOON!

Thank you to everyone who supported and purchased this workbook.

Special Thanks to Rebecca Reitz (rebeccareitz.com, @becca_reitz) for her beautiful artwork on the cover & pages 2, 10, 16, 20, 26, 29.

For a monthly subscription contact hello@spiritdaughter.com
or visit www.spiritdaughter.com

Disclaimer: The exercises and yoga sequences in this book are physical activities that should be performed carefully to avoid injury. You agree to accept all risks and release Spirit Daughter and any guest instructors from any and all liabilities. Please take care and enjoy.

Follow along our journey on IG:
@spiritdaughter

We always love seeing your photos & hearing about your experiences with the workbooks! Tag us to be featured on our community page:
@spiritdaughtercollective

Copyright © 2023 by Jill Wintersteen AKA Spirit Daughter

All rights reserved.

No part of this book may be reproduced or used in any manner without written permission of the copyright owner except for the use of quotations in a book review.

For more information contact:
hello@spiritdaughter.com.

First paperback edition September 2023

Book design by Rebecca Reitz
Cover design by Rebecca Reitz

ISBN 978-1-960013-34-7 (paperback)

www.spiritdaughter.com